Badger Publishing Limited
Oldmedow Road,
Hardwick Industrial Estate,
King's Lynn PE30 4JJ
Telephone: 01438 791037

www.badgerlearning.co.uk

4 6 8 10 9 7 5

Tiny but Deadly ISBN 978-1-78464-030-9

Text © John Townsend 2014
Complete work © Badger Publishing Limited 2014

Publisher: Susan Ross
Senior Editor: Danny Pearson
Publishing Assistant: Claire Morgan
Designer: Fiona Grant
Series Consultant: Dee Reid

Photos: Cover Image: Design Pics Inc/REX
Page 5: © Amazon-Images/Alamy
Page 6: © Kam Yee Fong/Alamy
Page 7: © ZUMA Press, Inc./Alamy
Page 8: © stuart thomson/Alamy
Page 9: © ephotocorp/Alamy
Page 11: © blickwinkel/Alamy
Page 12: © blickwinkel/Alamy
Page 15: © David Fleetham/Alamy
Page 18: © Matthijs Kuijpers/Alamy
Page 19: © Nature Picture Library/Alamy
Page 20: © imageBROKER/Alamy
Page 21: © Zoonar GmbH/Alamy
Page 22: © imageBROKER/Alamy
Page 23: © Roger Eritja/Alamy
Page 24: © Zoonar GmbH/Alamy
Page 25: © Phanie/Alamy
Page 26: © Akihito Yokoyama/Alamy
Page 28: © Maximilian Weinzierl/Alamy
Page 30: Getty/Shin.T

Attempts to contact all copyright holders have been made.
If any omitted would care to contact Badger Learning, we will be happy to make appropriate arrangements.

Contents

Vocabulary

arachnids   medical

creatures   milligram

deadliest   tropical

diseases   venom

The tiniest killers

Some of the deadliest animals on the planet are the smallest. If they sting or bite us we can be in big danger.

Some piranha fish are only ten centimetres long but they can do a lot of harm with their razor sharp teeth.

They hunt in shoals. If each little fish takes one bite, they can soon strip a body of its flesh.

1. LETHAL ARACHNIDS

The spider family (arachnids) can be a scary bunch of creepy crawlies. Lots of people are more afraid of spiders than any other 'mini-killers'.

Very few spiders are likely to kill you. But some can give you a nasty bite...

Black widow spider

The female black widow spider is not very big
(just 40 millimetres long) but it is deadly. She often kills
and eats the smaller male.

Her venom is strong but she only has a tiny amount of it.

If she bites you, it will feel like a pinprick and it might
make you feel ill for a couple of days.

Scary scorpions

Scorpions are also arachnids but they have a sting in their tail.

About 5000 people are killed by scorpion stings every year. Adults usually survive but children may not be so lucky.

Death stalker scorpions live in the deserts of Africa and the Middle East. They are yellow and about ten centimetres long.

The Indian red scorpion is tiny. It is only five to nine centimetres long so it can get into tiny spaces.

They like to hide in dark places during the day and people often find them in piles of clothes or in their shoes or beds!

Risky ticks

People think ticks are insects but they are like very tiny spiders – just three millimetres long. But they get bigger when they suck up your blood!

Tick facts:

1. There are about 850 types of tick.

2. Ticks feed on the blood of animals – such as your pets and you.

3. A tick bite can infect you with diseases that can make you very ill.

If you squeeze a tick when it is biting your skin, the germs get pushed into you through its mouth.

The best way to get the tick off is to grip it with tweezers close to the biting mouth and pull it off.

2: DEADLY SWIMMERS

Beware of what's in the water!

Meat-eating fish can be waiting to attack you in rivers and the sea.

Argentina – Christmas Day, 2013

It was a very hot day so hundreds of people went to cool down in the Parana River. They did not know it was full of piranhas.

The piranhas tore bits of flesh off the swimmers.

* More than 60 swimmers had deep cuts to their ankles and hands.

* Over 20 children were hurt.

* A seven-year-old girl lost part of a finger.

Blue-ringed octopus

The tiny blue-ringed octopus has one of the most deadly venoms in the world. A single milligram of its venom can kill you.

This octopus lives in the sea from Australia to Japan.

If you step on it – watch out! It can even bite through a wet suit.

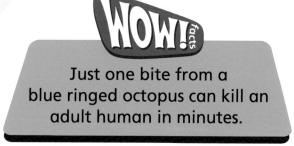

WOW! facts

Just one bite from a blue ringed octopus can kill an adult human in minutes.

When it is sleeping, the blue-ringed octopus is a brown colour.

The blue rings on its body only light up when it is in danger.

Don't pick one up! By the time you see the blue rings, it's too late!

Killer jellyfish

Every year people are killed by box jellyfish in the oceans of the world.

LUCKY TO BE ALIVE!

10-year-old Rachael Shardlow should be dead. A box jellyfish, stung her in Australia in 2009.

She was pulled from the water with the jellyfish still clinging to her legs but she lived through the attack.

She was very lucky as even a few milligrams of jellyfish venom can stop the heart.

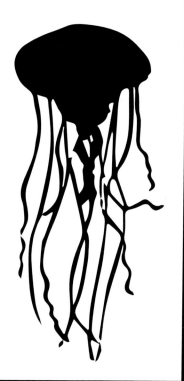

The Irukandji

The Irukandji is the smallest and most deadly jellyfish of all. Its venom is 100 times stronger than a cobra's. If you get stung, you get pain all over the body, sickness, sweating, a fast heart rate and a feeling you are going to die!

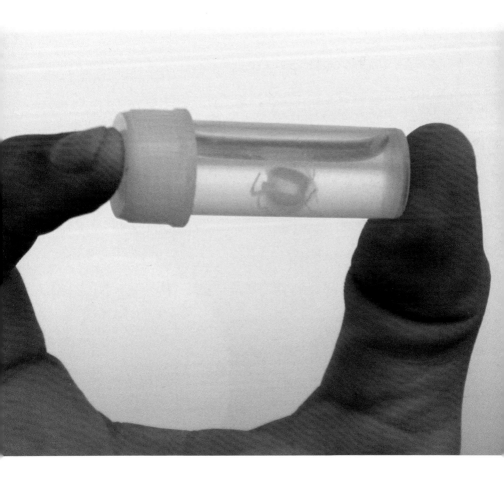

3. TOXIC RAINFOREST

In tropical swamps and forests, you can meet all sorts of tiny but deadly creatures.

Not all of them will bite or sting you. Some are lethal to touch.

Just licking your fingers after touching this tiny frog could kill you.

Killer frogs

The bright colours of the poison dart frogs of the Amazon are a warning to say: 'Keep away – I'm deadly.'

The strong toxin on their skin has been used by forest people in South America to poison the tips of blow-darts used in hunting.

WOW! facts

The golden poison frog is only four centimetres big but it has enough poison on its skin to kill up to 20 people.

Killer snakes

Africa's rainforests have some deadly snakes called mambas. There are green mambas as well as black mambas.

The black mamba is the fastest land snake in the world. It can move at up to 20 kilometres per hour. A single bite can inject enough deadly venom to kill 10-25 adults. A victim is likely to die within three hours unless medical help is at hand.

The green mamba is smaller than the black mamba. Its venom is weaker but, even so, one bite can kill you.

The good news is that it spends most of its time up trees – out of the way (unless you're a monkey).

Killer ants

Some forest insects are also scary.

The sting of the bullet ant is the most painful.
People say it's like being hit by a bullet.

In the Amazon rainforest the bullet ant is known as the
'24 hour ant' because its sting can last up to 24 hours.

There are many sorts of army ants – and they all have thousands of 'soldiers' that bite.

When they're on the move they will eat any living thing that gets in their way.

If you step on a nest or fall asleep near a nest, the soldier ants will swarm over you and you'll be eaten alive!

4. FATAL FLYERS

Have you ever been bitten by a mosquito?

The mosquito sucks up your blood and leaves you with an itchy spot.

In some parts of the world, mosquitos do a lot more harm.

One bite can kill you.

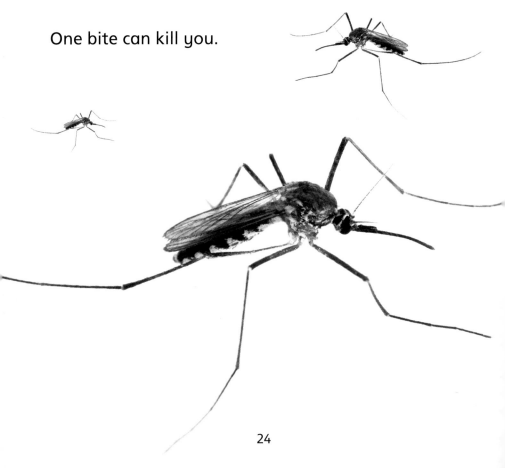

Mossie danger

Some mosquitoes carry deadly diseases. If one of these mosquitoes bites you, it can pass malaria into your blood.

Malaria kills almost two million people each year.

The mosquito can also infect you with other deadly diseases. Every year, 30,000 people die of yellow fever and 6000 die of West Nile virus.

That's a lot of deaths from a tiny insect.

Buzzing killers

A hornet is a type of wasp. Some Asian hornets have a very nasty sting.

The Asian hornet is three to four centimetres long – about the size of a human thumb.

It jabs its venom into you and your body can go into shock. Then you might die.

Asian hornets often make the news headlines:

2013 DEADLY HORNETS

Hornets have killed 42 people in China and injured more than 1500 with their powerful sting.

2014 DEADLY ASIAN HORNETS ON THEIR WAY

There are fears the Asian hornets that killed six people in France are on their way to the UK.

Killer bees

African honey bees can get a bit angry. If they feel under threat, they swarm and attack. Their stings can make some people really ill.

These bees are now found in America where they are called 'killer bees'.

SWARM OF KILLER BEES STINGS WOMAN 1000 TIMES

A woman was attacked by a swarm of 75,000 killer bees that covered her body. She disturbed a nest in Palm Desert, California.

A bee expert said, "They just went into her car and attacked her. They were mad."

The woman was taken to hospital to recover.

Some people are scared of big animals but it's often the little creatures that can cause the most harm.

Some of them, like the piranha or the blue-ringed octopus, live in faraway countries.

But some of them, like the deadly Asian hornet or the blood-sucking tick, are a bit closer to home.

They might be watching you right now!

Questions

How long are piranhas? *(page 5)*

Roughly how many people are killed by scorpion stings every year? *(page 8)*

What colour is the blue-ringed octopus when it is asleep? *(page 15)*

How many people can the poison on a golden poison frog's skin kill? *(page 19)*

In 2013, how many people did Asian hornets injure? *(page 27)*

Other than in Africa, where in the world are African honey bees found? *(page 28)*

INDEX